Poetic Colorations

AFTER THE RAIN

D HOLLAND

www.trafford.com
North America & international
toll-free: 1 888 232 4444 (USA & Canada)
fax: 812 355 4082

Contents

PART THREE
"BROKEN WITH PURPOSE"

PART FOUR
SUBSTANCE OF A WOMAN

PART FIVE
CHILDREN OF GOD

PART SIX
FAITH WALK

Reflections and Acknowledgements

Reflections

As I sit here ... my mind reflects back to fond memories of my sons. It seems like only yesterday and yet... it has been 28 years since I've seen their precious smiling faces. The pain of losing them in 1991

Has really never dissipated; it has only found a special place inside of me to go, where there is no light to shine upon it., I guess some people would agree with me that with time comes healing or at least you learn how to put your feelings towards death in its right prospective, looking at death from a spiritual & biblical prospective definitely helped me to cope all of these years. I know it was and still is the power of God that has kept me going this far in my life.

Through my faith in the Lord Jesus Christ, it has given me hope of experiencing the life here after, when I will see my sons again. This book is not only a memorial to my sons, Monte' and DJ, but it is also a memorial to the memory of my dearest little friend "Michael" who helped me to cope with my loss, when I didn't know how to cope, 6 year old little Michael unfortunately passed away too soon after our acquaintance. Also in loving memory of my parents; John & Naomi who instilled within me the values of Christ and his promises through his word. In memory of George my father's first cousin and a friend, you will always be loved and remembered for your wisdom of the word of God and your deep love for your family.

In memory of my dearest eldest sister, Camilla, who taught me how to be joyful in my tribulation, In memory of my loving sister Ardelia the family protector and the out spoken sister, you are missed Sis. In memory of my grandmother, Christine Vinson, who laid down the spiritual foundation of faith and bible truth for all of her off spring of many generations to come, she will always remain an inspiration and a pillar of faith in all of our lives.

Special Acknowledgements

I thank God for allowing this book to give birth.

Special acknowledgements to my, confidant, lover, prayer partner and greatest supporter, my handsome talented husband, Maurice, I know God placed you in my life to love me and to help me through my healing process because you have stuck with me through the storms of my life. You have supported me with my writing projects and various ministries throughout the years, by created illustrations, taking photographs and you created this beautiful book cover and I love you with all of my heart and I thank God for you.

Special acknowledgements to my beautiful, gifted daughters Camilla and Dee for hanging in there through the rough times and even when y'all wanted to give up on life, you hung in there! I know sometimes life was hard for y'all, even through our ups and downs, love is the glue that has kept us together; I know there was times when I thought you girls were giving up, but praise God! I'm so proud of y'all strength and perseverance and academic achievements! Love y'all girls so much.

A special shout out to my beautiful granddaughters, Kaila'na little ballerina and Saylana buttercup y'all both will always hold a special place in Grammy's heart. A shout out to my daughter Tara, her husband Brian and their kids, our two older grand kids, Britney and Marquis, much love to you all. Britney (my granddaughter) thanks for modeling for the front cover of this book. You are

So beautiful and talented and I am so very proud of you!

Special Acknowledgement also to my sister Beverly (I call my twin). Thanks Sis for walking with me through this thing. In my darkest hour... I will forever be grateful to you, your kids and your husband, Sis y'all gave me a place of refuge when I was homeless and you fed me when I could not eat, bathe me when I could not bathe, cried with me in my darkest rain. You are truly my beautiful soul sister and I love you. I thank my siblings, and my family for supporting me through my storms.

A special shout out to Kimberly my lovely talented niece thank you for your wonderful foreword in this book, your words of encouragement resonate with me and I will carry them in my heart forever. Love you.

This book was not written for the purpose of earthly wealth or to gain any notoriety but, that the words on the pages may enrich someone's life. My goal is to try and help someone to get through, what I have already been through and what I'm still going through as I heal and also to give them a renewed prospective on life through every poem of testimony and experience, of my journey and my views on life. I pray everyone reading this book will be blessed by it to be a blessing to someone else. May God bless the reader of this book and keep you in his loving care.

The Author

Foreword, by Kimberly Jones

Now, I know that you'll say that it was not you, but God, I do agree, but what I mean to say here is that whatever God does in anyone's life, he does not force anyone's will.

I mean that in everybody's lives however different, however difficult or easy, everybody makes choices that control their ultimate fates.

That's my personal belief. I believe that individual everyday choices we make put us on different paths to some end, so we choose.

That being said, it seemed and sometimes (often) still seems as if life has not been at all easy for you. I'm not in your skin to know but it looks like it's been one thing after another, and not small things, but Big things...the kind of events that some people never recover from, because it's not the initial blows, but the days and years that follow and the lasting effects. And yet, you are not pitiful at all.

So right now, I feel simply in awe because you are not broken. Your life has not become a funeral for all of your losses.

You often remind me of what strength looks like. Every now and then, I think about you, because you are worth thinking about. In spite of anything bad that happens, you choose to go on to move forward, to get up if you've been knocked down.

Not only do you choose to continue, but you do it triumphantly! As if there was never another option. I find this amazing about you. I'll bet I'm not the only one you inspire, but I can only speak for myself. I am inspired by you and I thought you should know.

Introduction

One night my brother Mark had a dream...

The setting of his dream took place in the house we grew up in as kids many years ago. On a sunny day there was sleeping me. My brother explained that I was in a most aberrant place to rest; I was in the basement of the house on a small uncomfortable cot. He said, I was in such a peaceful sleep he did not bother to wake me.

But as he started out of the house and headed up the street towards the store the sky turned dark gray. Large clouds formed in the sky and lightning flashed and it started thundering and it was followed by heavy down pours. The down pours were so extreme that he said that he could not walk any further without struggle so he was seeking shelter, but just then he said he remembered me and the fact that one of the windows was open upstairs in the house. My brother Mark said he knew within his heart that I didn't stand a chance to survive this rain. He looked up to the sky and said, "God please save her" and the tears poured out of his eyes intermingled with the rain down his wet clothes. Just then the rain stopped instantaneously! Mark said "Thank you God" and immediately turned around and began to run back home to our house, he said even though the streets were flooded with water he ran anyway trying to get back home help to me.

On his way home he said he was praying and asking God to please save my life even though he believed I was gone. As he passed by our neighbors they were dumping buckets of water from their homes into the streets because no one knew this storm was coming therefore, they were unprepared. When he arrived out of breath at our front door of the house it was flooded. He ran around the back alley way to the back yard of the house because he knew he could go down the basement stairs to enter the area of the house where I was asleep when he had left me earlier. He swallowed and gasped and whispered a prayer for what he was about to see, knowing that I was in the bottom of the house he figured I was drowned for real and he thought I didn't wake up to get out in enough time.

My brother said he slowly opened the basement door from the outside and water poured out into the back yard and on him. He opened it a little more and water continued to gush out. He pulled it wide open and jumped to the side of the steps that led down stairs and looked from afar to allow the water to run out and to his surprise he said he was shocked at what he saw, Mark said he slowly walked back down the steps and witnessed the weirdest thing he ever saw in his life.

(Continued)

He said the cement basement floor was drenched with water and water dripping from upstairs down onto the furniture but there I was still fast asleep laying on the cot in the middle of the basement floor and all around my cot was a complete circle of dry floor and under my cot was completely dry as well and so was I and all inside of the inner circle around my sleeping area. Not a drop of water was on me or my covers and I slept as though nothing had happened at all. As he was sharing his dream my brother was lying in his hospital bed with his thin frail and weak body due to a grave illness at the time of his dream and after he finished sharing all of the details of his dream he looked up at me with inquisitiveness in his tired weak eyes from his hospital bed and asked; "Hey Sis, what's up with you anyway?" I answered, "What do you mean" As I stood in awe of his dream about me.

Mark asked, "Why did I dream that about you Sis?" "I said to him, I think even though you're on your sick bed that you are worried about me because of my great loss that just happened, I think the Lord gave you this dream to ensure you that he is with me with me through all I'm going through and my brother as far as what the meaning of your dream is, it sounds like God gave me calm in my storm.

God placed his hedge of protection around me and encircled me during that storm that no harm would come to me. Even though everything else was flooded out and ruined all around me. I said to him the same way God kept me in the midst of that terrible storm, he will keep you calm through this illness and he will heal your body. I believe there was a message of encouragement in that dream for both of us my brother.

Reflecting back It was very interesting to me for my brother to have this dream and to remember it, because anyone who knows my brother can tell you, that he has always had a terrible memory and secondly he was in the hospital very ill and a little sedated with meds so his drowsiness should have prevented the remembrance of it all. My sister Beverly and I were there together at the hospital to visit him sitting at his bedside and praying for his healing at the time and encouraging him to hang on. The irony of it all was that I had just experienced a fatal tragedy of great loss a few months prior to his hospitalization. God sent a message of love to me through my brother's dream that everything would be alright.

That divine message God sent me was received with an open heart and humble gratefulness. I felt comforted knowing that God heard my prayers and had not forgotten me during my time of pain and loss. God also heard our prayers of healing for our brother.

Mark was healed, praise God! Mark lives today with his loving wife and they now have 3 beautiful daughters and 6 wonderful grandchildren he continues to give God honor and praise for saving his life and allowing him to live.

And to see his all of kid's graduate high school and two elder kids graduate college and he had the privilege to escort his youngest daughter to her prom as her date in 2014. My brother dream inspired my book subtitle **"After the rain"**, and helped me to find that rainbow through the poetic colorations of my life experiences and God helped me to see a brand new prospective through his dream and his desire to save his baby sister from drowning in the rain. Thank you Mark for inspiring the introduction of this book and for being a great brother..... I love you.

Part One

After The Rain

RE-SIL-TENCE

(Definition- The capacity to recover quickly from difficulties; toughness)

After my storm…there came isolated showers with personification of my poetic colorations
Splattered onto the empty canvas walls of my wounded soul

It was deeply imbedded pain and…

I was indubitably feeling this thing let me explain

It was too many and so many back to back to back disappointments and hard hits that my poor mind could not fathom it.

It was so surreal that it just couldn't be for real

The kind of feeling that makes you down right ill

And could lead you to OD on pills, or make you so anxious you just can't keep still.

I felt like I was suffering from **PTSD** (*Post trauma stress disorder*) anxiously waiting the unknown sitting there in the stress zone

I wanted to give up on my life because the pain was just too much for me to bear

But God sustained me and helped me from heading into the bottomless pit

I thank God because I was almost there…

Expressions of my life colorations are emotionally connected to events and experiences giving me an outlet and it have also brought me healing and somehow I have as a butterfly divulged into my new birth.

I find comfort in free expression which is a release of positive energy and validation for my own self worth.

I am not focused on what hurt me in the past, but I have learned the lessons of what my painful pass has taught me and one thing for sure, my past has taught me to love even harder

I am determined not to let the devil win. I asked God to carry me through this, for I could not do it on my own.

"How could I bounce back from total devastation?" One bad thing after the next just as brother Job in the bible experienced. *(Job 1: 1-19)*

I asked God "How....Why....and "what exactly just happened?"

There was no way I could wrap my mind around this and accept the pill I had to swallow and the hand fate had dealt me but somehow through the grace and mercy of God and only through his strength....I did!

Now I live to tell the story! Thanks be to God! I glorify you my Lord the sustainer of my mind, body and soul!

"Let this mind be in you, which is also in Christ Jesus." (Philippians 2:5)

"In Loving Memory of My Sons"

My Tribute
A Psalm of love for my sons Monte' and DJ

I can almost smell the faint aroma of sweet cinnamon and vanilla extract as the fragrance fills the room with your presence of love. Fond memories of your handsome smiling little faces as I picture you draped in fine white linen and your hair in black curly locks and small glittering crowns of gold with diamonds upon your heads. Within my heart you are very much alive; you are not dead. I can envision you dancing upon the clouds above. I can almost see the dew drops falling down from those clouds into a pond filled with white swans and pink rose petals and as each dewdrop hit the waters, reflections of your heavenly glow over shadows the waters and fills the sky with a rainbow, that reflects all of your colors of love. In my mind, I see you with Jesus in Heaven, wrapped in his gentle arms of sugar coated, sweet gum drops, dipped into the honey comb flavor of the Father's everlasting love.

Monte' and DJ in my heart you are not gone, but instead your memory lives and motivates me to have a purpose in this life, for I know one day, not far way, I will see you again and then we will reunite and rejoice and we shall do the dance of triumph and victory before Jesus and his Father in heaven… together.

With all my love,

(Your mother, until we meet again, you shall forever be in my heart and I will love you until the end of time.)

I would like to share this scripture with you in reference to what the Bible (KJV) says about death, and also to let you know that this poem is comforting to my heart and this is my personal vision of my babies, and I thank God for these comforting thoughts, but I know that it will be as the Bible says, for now my boys are asleep in Christ. In these promised words of scripture the Lord shares with us that on that great getting up morning, when Jesus Christ returns for his all of his children. All glory and praise and honor will be to our king Jesus Christ!

"For the Lord himself shall descend from heaven with a shout, with the voice of the archangel, and the trump of God: and the dead in Christ shall rise first: Then we which are alive and remain shall be caught up together with them in the clouds to meet the Lord in the air: and so shall we ever be with the Lord.

"Wherefore comfort one another with these words." (I Thessalonians 4:16-18)

This book would not have been possible without the undying love that I still hold within my heart for my children. They shall never be forgotten, as long as their memory still burns so deeply within my heart.

All of my love, Mother

QURPLE SPARROW

There once was a purple sparrow
Unique in all her ways
She flew below the dark rain clouds with a heavy heart most days
And all the skies above were gray
Within her heart she believed that she could fly so high…but she
was sore afraid until one day the purple sparrow had the courage
to pray…
Then the wind began to blow under her wings
Then the wind began to roar
Her body started to shift and the wind blew under her fragile
wings once more.
Then the purple sparrow began to fly…..then she began to soar
Way up high above the gray rain clouds that weighed her down
no more
She flew up so high she could barely see the ground and she felt
no pain
Tears of gratitude overflowed dropping down along with the
monsoon rain
Finally, the little purple sparrow courage again regained
All storm clouds disappeared and the sun shined again
And there resting on her feathers was a emit glow reflecting colors
of a rainbow.

> *"But they that wait upon the Lord shall renew their strength;
> they shall mount up with wings as eagles; they shall run and
> not be weary; and they shall walk, and not faint".
> (Isaiah 40:31 KJV)*

AFTER THE RAIN

Walking in the dampness of evening
Broken hearted and seeking solace of peace
Coming forth an expulsion of teardrops from my eyes
Was falling down into my reflection
Into a rain puddle around my feet
The literal rain has ceased to come again... I don't know exactly when
Considering the storm that I felt deep within
Distorted vision and my heavy heart mourned
That day for me was the beginning of my internal storm
How could God expect for me to want to live...on?
Mental flash backs of my sons and the pain of my loss...
It was right then that I remembered how Jesus carried the weight of the cross.
Trying to imagine just how his father must have felt deep down inside
As he witnessed his only begotten son, nailed to the cross, as he suffered, bled and died...oh! The outpouring of tears the Father must have cried!
Who can feel the empathy of a mother's pain? Or understand her cries in the darkness of her rain? Who can understand her sleepless nights and painful grieving tears? Perhaps a mother's prayer has reached the Father's ears.
Maybe he reflected back to Calvary when he made the ultimate sacrifice, of sending his only son Jesus
So that we might live by giving of his son's precious holy life.

> "He makes the storm calm, so that the waves thereof
> are still"
> Psalms {107:29}

I Got Lifted

I decided to live today
My spirit was filled within me
My cup ran over
It spilled over until the room was filled
At that moment time stood still

I got lifted

Tears streaming down
No more need to frown
Feet started dancing
I couldn't sit down

I got lifted

I didn't get tired
My spirit was on fire
My heart got inspired

I got lifted

Joy unspeakable spoke in volume
It was astounded
My lips offered praise
On my Hallelujah Day

God got lifted

> *Jesus said; "And if I be lifted up from the earth, will draw
> all men unto me."*
> *(John 12:32) (KJV)*

TELL IT

Preacher commissioned
Feed God sheep
Impart the word
Say what they never heard

Preacher Tell it

Straight and Narrow road
Sinner repent
Lay down your heavy load

Preacher Tell it

Lost your way
Found new faith today
Though they criticize and keep tellin lies
Go on sinner and get baptized

Preacher Tell it

New life has begun
Your victory is won
Sinner now you go tell it

> *Enter ye in at the strait gate: for wide is the gate, and broad is the way, that leadeth to destruction, and many there be which go in there. Because strait is the gate, and narrow is the way, which leadeth unto life, and few there be that find it.*
> *(Matthew 7:13- 14) (KJV)*

Part Two

In This Struggle
To Win

Don't Give Up/ Keep it Moving

You have come too far to turn around
Just look back at your journey
And see how far you have climbed
Measure the distance before you
With what's left behind…

Just keep on climbing
Don't dawdle back at your yesterdays
Remember lots wife
She lagged and regretted leaving what was gone
She never had the blessing of moving on
Each new day is a new beginning
A new opportunity to reach your goal
If you keep looking back
You just might block your blessing
And hinder new horizons from progressing

So remember
No regrets keep looking up
One day that door of opportunity will swing open
So, don't worry about the one behind you that was shut

> *"And let us not be weary in well doing: for in due season
> we shall reap, if we faint not." (Galatians 6:9)*

STAND TALL IN THE FACE OF ADVERSITY AND SQUASH YOUR LEMONS

Life is very perplexed and it throws many lemons (*problems, trials etc.,*) our way.

It's how we respond to the lemons in our lives that makes all of the difference.

Some say, turn your lemons into lemonade and I definitely agree.

But let's do better than that and douse in it!

Think about it? Without adversity in our lives we would never know peace.

It's so apprehensible to see the lemon (*Life stumbling blocks*) but not as simple to look at it in the face and shout "I will not allow you to have victory over my life!

This is only if there is a new perspective and a new take on it, then we can stand tall on and in our faith with confidence and squash those sour lemons!

The idea is even when you're feeling down trotted, weak and weary go on and make the lemonade and worry about the sweetener later. Sometimes you don't get sweetness after victory (*scars*) until they heal (*the after math*) but you get confidence in knowing scars and all that you won the battle because it didn't break you. There are areas of my life that I'm still growing in and have not fully overcome but I exercise faith daily through prayer and in the hope that one day I will fully overcome my issues through the help of Christ.

> *"My grace is sufficient for thee: for my strength is made perfect in weakness. Most gladly therefore will I rather glory in my infirmities, that the power of Christ may rest upon me (KJV 2 Corinthians 12:9)" The spirit is indeed willing but the flesh is weak (Matthew 26:41).*

You see, the idea of squeezing that lemon is the key to conquering your giant or giants.

I encourage you to mentally try it. You will find renewed strength and then realize your problems don't control you in fact you have control over how you respond to your problems. No we can't prevent negative things from happening to us but our response to them determines if problems will break us or make us. Look at the bright side of every situation believe me there is a bright side somewhere in it.

Sometimes life obstacles are bitter sweet and some just plain bitter, even after we fully overcome them.

If we focus on the victory, our lemons will no longer have power over our lives anymore, spilling sour juice into our lives.

Yes, unexpected occurrences do happen to all of us but once you get over the initial blow

Pray and regroup. The bible says, "Let this mind be in you which was also in Christ Jesus"

(KJV Phil. 2:5)

This means to use your spiritual mind to overcome the carnal obstacles around you.

The theory "Mind over Matter" works.

Blind faith of knowing God is with you is comforting.

> *2 Corinthians 5:7) ("For we walk by faith not by sight" (Hebrews 11:6) – (without faith it impossible to please God.)*

In Honor of my Ancestors / God has not Forgotten His Precious Black Stones

"But, you are a chosen people, a royal priesthood, a holy nation, God's special possession, that you may declare the praises of him who called you out of darkness into his wonderful light". (1 Peter 2:9)

God has not Forgotten/ Precious Black Stones

In the depth of the slave ship
Where no light could be found
There were precious black stones
Stones that once was, but had not...a voice

Stolen, Beaten, downtrodden, and thought to be nothing
But God had not forgotten
Refined and purified through the trials of fire
They had only but one desire to be set free and only one faith and
hope in their God
Many were cast aside and disregarded their true value unseen
Their oppressors saw them as cursed, undesired, sold them as
property, and called them unclean
But God had not forgotten; For to God, they were his precious
black stones worth far more than the white man could see
If only they could put aside hatred, prejudice and see their true
abilities
I'm so glad God had not forgotten...and from their bondage he set
them free
God being the chief corner stone that the builders rejected full of
grace and mercy could feel their pain and their struggles, he heard
their cries for deliverance...and now today,
We are the off spring and the voices of those stones, so I say to
you... Precious- Black - Stones
Rise up and stand!

For we are worth far more than rubies and diamonds and we are
more valuable than any man can see but because the struggle
ain't over yet, we must continue to stand on our faith and always
remember...our God has not forgotten.

Ain't no Blessing in Oppression

Dry place
Rich soil
Dark past
Burdened toil
Night Cries
Screamin' beatins
Raped by hate
Ain't no Escape

Hush up
Git da' workin'
Da' master cumin'
Gonna get a whippin'
If sommin' git a missin'

Mummer cookin, cleanin' washin'
Nursin' da' masta babies cleanin'up their mess
Workin in the da' field
Ain't gettin' no rest
Workin' hard night in day
Her babies hungry
Treated like trash ya throw away
God gonna have da' last say

Datty can't say nothin'
He called a boy
Had to watch his lil girl taken
By da' masta son Roy

Granny in da' field
Get reel ill
Sun burn skin
Bury and replaced by next of kin

Mummer and Datty tired
Workin in da' cotton fields wit' plantation scarred hands
Prayin' to da' good Lawd to be free from da' masta bloody
cursed lan

Who Told You That?

Who said you're not beautiful?

Who told you that?

Who told you to frown and hang your head down because you're
black?

Who told you that your ugly cause' your skin is black like coal?
Who said you will never ever in this life reach your potential or
goal?
Who told you that your hair is too hard, coarse and nappy?
And that your ancestors were worthless black slaves and you will
never be happy?
Then called you ignorant cause' their rude insults made you get a
little snappy?

Who told you what you are, who you are,
What's your worth?
What you ain't?
Where you're going and what you can't?

Who told you that?

Beloved don't listen to the lies they tell
They dug a hole of despair for you but instead they fell
Lift up your beautiful black head and know this well
You are a precious polished diamond created by God above
Take confidence in knowing black child that you are loved
I just came to remind you of this very known fact... they can't tell
you nothing
'Bout you're black.

$\mathcal{D}$AUGHTER OF A $\mathcal{K}$ING

They persecute me and treat me unfair… could it be my honey brown skin or my kinky hair?
Giving me the unwanted desk and the broken down chair
Maybe they really don't know… I'm the daughter of a King?
They set me up for failure, right from the start, with no integrity and no heart. Giving me no flexibility only limitations; they have no compassion and certainly no consideration
And they ain't offering me any special accommodations, but believe me, they have very high expectations

Maybe they really don't know the greatness within me, because I'm the daughter of a Mighty King!
They talk about me and put me down but I'm not going to let them steal my starry crown, you see… no weapons formed against me shall prosper they can only fail for the love of God shall always prevail!
The pressure can't break me nor shake me
Knowing my Heavenly Father will not forsake me
Even though the enemy is attempting to over take me

I don't worry about it…Because I know; I'm the daughter of a King
Rejected by his own, nowhere to lay his head he felt all alone
His parents could not find a place to call home

Sadly the world did not know, he was the King of Kings
Mary carrying the Holy Savior in her womb when her labor pains began
But the people continued to say… there's no more room in the Inn
They rejected the Heavenly King, the only one who could forgive their sins

How disheartening to know the cold hearts of men, not allowing the love of God to come in, they heard of whom he was but minds could not comprehend…The were in the very presence of the King The babe born in a manger, the great teacher who fed the poor, healed the sick, and raised the dead and who was crucified and died on Calvary cross for their sins was the SON OF GOD…but maybe perhaps, they really didn't want to know… that they were the children of the King.

(Proverbs 31: 29-30) Many daughters have done virtuously, but thou excel them all.
Favor is deceitful, and beauty is vain: but a woman that fears the Lord, she shall be praised.

Silent Write

Can you hear me write? If you missed it
Here is the follow-up review from the critics corner stew
I heard words of promise filled with hope
Wrote with passion in every stroke
Some spoke of struggles, anger and pain's yoke
Some words were so strong they could even make you choke
Seriously... no joke

Can anybody hear me?
Can my words be heard?
I write through my passion in every silent word
Some are so tight ...yeah, you heard me that's right
So tight cause' it's my silent write

No discussion or no rhetorical follow through
This brief written review will have to do
Compliments from the critic's corner stew
With some tasty rhymes of silent writes for you to chew.

> *(James 1:19) "Wherefore, my beloved brethren, let every*
> *man be swift to hear, slow to speak, slow to wrath."*
> *"Silence is golden and full of wisdom"*

WARFARE

Sleepless nights
No strength to fight
Evil don't wait to come out at night
It's so crazy people are killing folks when it's day light
They don't seem to discern wrong from right
It doesn't matter whether you live in Howard County, or Park Heights

Murder on the streets of Baltimore every day
Gun violence is taking young lives away
We are crying out please! No more killing in Baltimore
Kids aren't safe at our schools, on the street not even on their own front porch what is all this violence for?
It's so bad out here it's too dangerous for grown folks to go out to the grocery store

Senseless gunfire is a relentless enemy to humanity
Causing the loss of many lives and endless insanity
It's a very serious issue growing daily and its bitter hatred never retires
Every moment of our lives so precious
The chance of losing it is dire

Let's pull together and spread the message of love and unity, stay vigilant, pray for one another and show that we care
It's time to wake up y'all this thing is for real its spiritual warfare!

> *"For the weapons of our warfare are not carnal, but mighty through God*
> *To the pulling down of strong holds"*
> *(2 Corinthians 10:4 KJV)*

Part Three

"Broken with Purpose"

"He heals the broken in heart, and bind up their wounds"
(Psalms 147:3)

WHAT COLOR IS YOUR LOVE?

What color is your love? You said Purple, Black, and Blue?
If you really think that's love, then God help you! Cause' you sure
have a distorted view!
What sweet things does it whisper in your ear? Does it sound like
put downs, fault finding, insults that makes you more depressed,
than you're aware? Oh, yeah...

Don't forget the other stuff...
You know.... The stuff that I can't even say up in here
Then it has the nerve to whisper... I didn't mean it, I'm sorry; you
know how much I love you and how much I really do care.
Do you like it when it calls you out of your name...demean you
and make you feel ashamed?

Let me ask you...What color is your pain? A purple bruise that
aches so badly with no sign of relief...and all your love wants do
is give you more and more grief....

I want to know...how many more beatings?
And how long you gonna weep?
Let go of this love, before your 6 feet deep.

What will it take to admit your mistake and release this colored
love of hate?
It don't mean you no good... believe me I can truly relate
Life is too short and real love doesn't hurt or hate...it heals and it
protects
So what you gonna do....live in fear? What's next?

You say the colors of your love are Purple Black and blue?
Well, I'm a little bit confused, cause' when I look at you...
...I only see black... Cause' child, all the lights in your house just
went out...
And so did you...

On The Other Side

Domestic Abuse does not only happen to women but men experience abusive situations too.

After interviewing and taking notes from some men that went through some bad experiences, I compiled all of it together into this poem that expresses my view of what could possibly be from a man's perspective.

FROM A MAN'S PERSPECTIVE

From a man's perspective I can give you my take
On this topic of male abuse coming from men who loved chicks
With control issues and said… this was their first big mistake!
They didn't see it coming unto Ms. Crazy arrived at the door
With a crow bar in her hand
Looking for war
Insecure and accusing
She thought infatuation was love and her language was quite abusing
But he didn't find it flattering or a bit amusing?
Looking for the first train out town
Cause' she acting crazy
Then she said you ain't leaving me, cause' I'm having your baby
You better put a ring on it
You know all you want is me; I'm your only desire
No…He said I don't think so
And the chick slashed his brand new tires
When confronted
She attacked him cursing with a blade
Then she pressed charges
And showed up at court lying in her Versace gold designer shades
Men learn this valuable lesson taught from our experiences we share
She's a female Looking fine in all her glory but be aware…
Before you say this chick is mine, because she might not be so kind
And because she's a female
Ain't anybody going believe you're a victim of her abuse? And you might be the one that end up in jail.

COMPLETION

Through trials she struggled smiling behind a mask
Searching for answers to questions to painful to ask

Mental struggles within her own mind
Seeking refuge but it she could never find
The missing pieces held within her heart now open wide

No longer blind cause now all is seen
Finally the time has come for her to be free
Released from her own walls of captivity

Her soul not withholding but ready to give
Finally she had a real reason to live
Dancing in the liberation of her rain... no more struggles... numb
to the pain

All fear is gone, no longer broken... her spirit is lifted and her
mind is wide open.

No More Stripes

By his stripes we are healed
Humiliation and agitation crushed by the weight
Anguish and pain endured
Treated unfair and then beat some more
Enemy thought he had the score
Whipped and betrayed by his own
Devil thought he had his throne

Rose up one morning
Conquered death
Stripes diminished
Enemy was defeated no longer a threat
Coming one day soon in all of his Kingly glory
Nail prints in his hands will tell his story
Paid the price for our ransom with his love sacrifice
Gonna wear a crown and robe no more stripes

$\mathcal{V}$ALUE

ONE SHINY PENNY
ROLLS DOWN THE GUTTER
NO ONE CARES
CAUSE' THEY GOT MORE BUTTER

PENNY RUST
NOONE TO TRUST
DARK AND DIRTY
YEARS PASS ABOUT THIRTY

CORRODED AND AGED
THE WHITE WASHED PENNY
IS FOUND IN IT'S LAST STAGE

TAKEN IN CLEANED AND SHINED
THAT PENNY IS JUST LIKE MAN KIND
LOST AND IN THE GUTTER
NO ONE CARES
UNTIL A GOOD SAMARITAN
COMES FROM NO WHERE

SHOWING THE LOVE OF GOD
TO THOSE WHO ARE DOWN TROTTEN
AND HAVE LOST THEIR WAY

NOT WORRIED ABOUT WHAT OTHERS SAY
TAKING THE TIME TO HELP SOMEONE
NURTURE, FEED, CLOTHE, TEACH AND PRAY.

(MATTHEW 25:40)
"In as much as ye have done unto the least of these my brethren, ye have done it unto me".

PART FOUR

SUBSTANCE OF A WOMAN

PARENTHOOD

Parenthood is challenging and can sometimes be taxing.
Our children go through stages at different ages and every child is different and unique, there are none just alike. I have learned through my parenting experience that negative and positive exposure and various life experiences when they are growing up truly effect children in diverse ways, It effects how they think and overall how they develop.
Life can either make or break them.

There were precious moments with my kids when they have been right down adorable! And other times they have been a pain… if you know what I mean? Though I love them never the less.

I found in the inception of my parenting experience that sometimes dealing with my living children has been more painful than dealing with the grief of those that I loss. In my case losing children to death in correlation to losing my grip on my living children has been very painful at times.
I'm still learning how to let them go and how to allow them to be the adults they are now.
It's not easy, and Lord knows I'm not a perfect mom. I never have been and never will be the **"ideal"** mom. I just do the best that I can to show my children that I love them.

In all honesty the stress I gave my mother has come back to haunt me. The advice my mother gave to me would have prevented my heartache and abuse, if I had only heeded to her warnings, life could have been a lot better for me and my kids. I've learned that experience is the best teacher and also that **"Mother knows best"** well in my mother's case it was the truth! I truly miss my mother and all of our talks.

There was a time when after losing my sons I felt like my living kids were gone.

I thought they were leading lives of destruction in their past and it was devastating to me as a mother.

The journey has been a long tiresome one. I had to acknowledge the fact that my loss affected my children in ways I didn't see in the earlier years.

Exposing them to abusive situations and they were trying to cope with grieving as children this was rough on them.

My divorce and being a single working mom was exacerbating for them when they were kids.

They needed more of me coming up but I had to stand in the gap and take care and provide for their physical needs. This does not excuse me from anything but it it's just the truth.

If I could turn back the hands of time I probably would have done things a lot differently.

God granted me the opportunity to become a grandparent and it's been a blessing but it has also had it challenges, but I love being a grandparent.

I have fought all of my children lives to protect them and now that same love and protective nurturing nature is there for my grand children. It's been a journey of healing for all of us as a family.

All of my struggles with parenting and trying to maintain my life as a single parent and work full-time job have been a lot. Many times I have asked the Lord, "Is this barren land?" I cannot begin to explain it all, but I'm so grateful to the Lord that my girls have achieved academically and have matured into the lovely young women they are today. My eldest was just baptized and renewed her walk with God and for this alone I am so grateful. This is a very important and vital part of my life walking with God, so for my daughter to make this commitment it means the world to me.

My youngest is the bible scholar; she loves the word of God and can talk about the bible for hours and her interpretation of the holy word. We have had great discussions about the bible.

I instilled the word of God and Christian values in my children from the very beginning of their lives. They know the truth and they must decide on their own if they choose to serve the Lord or not, it's their right to choose not mine.

All I can say is that the Lord has carried me through the most difficult devastating times in my life when I thought I could not carry on. Raising my kids he was there guiding my footsteps and helping me to stay sane through all of the insanity surrounding me. There were health issues, when I could not move my hands to comb my hair without having severe pain and a time I thought I would be cripple due to a physical disability and unable to function independently and personal issues that the enemy (devil) tried his best to use to drown me and overtake me but God gave me a inner strength that I cannot explain that would not allow me give up. I have weathered the storms of life but only by his strength and his grace and mercy not on my own. You see, I know where my help comes from and it's from the Lord that made the heaven and the earth, he is to me, El Shaddai, God Almighty, Jehovah-Jireh, my provider, Jehovah-Rapha, my healer. God is everything to me.

I'm also grateful for my precious granddaughters they make me smile daily. They call me and Poppy frequently and always have something sweet to say to us. I thank God for my off spring. I know that my womb is blessed, they devil is a liar. To my daughters and grandchildren I leave you with a legacy of experience and my personal views to learn from my experiences and to never give up on God. Don't let your past or anyone else's opinion define you, but allow your past to change you into the beautiful person the Lord created you to be, find strength from your mistakes and keep your head up. Just know your momma is always praying for you and I love you so much. I pray the Lord blessings cover you.

Is This Barren Land?

How can a fertile womb be barren?
Or mothers grieve the living seed of her womb?
How can her living seed get trapped inside their own mental tomb?
If to live is for Christ, and to die is gain"
Then to give birth to a life that won't live right, is a life never lived
and a death in vain

Like the dust from the earth blows away with the wind;
Precious time wasted dissipates and life never begins.
Why Lord? Why? "Is there venom in my womb? Have any survived?
My womb is empty, cold and desolate and cries with despair
In this dry and barren land"

Have the sins of my youth trickled down into the blood of my off
spring and tainted my seed?

When I'm praying down on my knees does God hear my cries of
infertility?
Is there hope for my empty vessels to be filled with the living
water so their blind eyes can see? Or do they desire a cup filled
with rebellion, poisoning any hope of eternity? Lord please save
my children from self-destruction."

Daughter have I Told You Lately?

Daughter have I told you lately that I love you?

I cherish memories of you when you were only two

Cute as a baby doll and very talkative all of the time

Asking a million questions, reciting ABC's, reading Cat in the Hat aloud and singing your nursery rhymes

I remember taking you with me on daily bus trips

And you would say some things that would make me
Smile and talk through clenched teeth and say…Shhh…Child! Zip up them little lips!

You were quite the little whiz kid when you first started school back in the day
Even on summer vacation you would challenge your cousins on math and demand an answer and they would say,

Its summertime leave us alone, you just smiled and said, I don't think y'all knew the answer anyway!

I remember those straps with buckles fastened across the side of your red little shoes; colorful tights, large ruffled socks, two pony tails with ribbons, a front missing tooth, and baby dolls and build it blocks

Have I told you lately that I admire you for all of the achievements and growth you made?

If I haven't, I want you to know your mother loves you and in my heart you will always stay.

To my inquisitive child

Mommy No Wins

Arms folded
Pouted lips
Curly pony tail
Upset over a bag of chips
Had to have it your way
No shorts
All or nothing
Give you what you want
Or there really isn't any point?
Ice cream soda ginger ale pop
Loved playing a game of hop scotch
Dinner time child
Time to come in
Convincing you to do so
Mommy no wins
All grown up
Got your own stuff
Now you have kids too
Cute and adorable and stubborn just like you
Don't want to obey anything you say
Love to play outside with their friends
Dinner time children
Time to come in
Convincing them to do
Mommy no wins

To my beautiful daughter, Mommy Loves you stubborn and all
So proud of the obstacles you have overcome and the achievements you have
made. Hang in there parenting gets better with time

LITTLE FEET

Little feet
Playing hide n seek
Wanting to know
How many days are left in the week?
We can't wait to go to Red Robins to eat
Trying to walk in poppy's big boots
We got to take a picture of this Honey
She's too darn cute!
Placing tiaras on top of poppy's head
In the kitchen mixing, dipping helping Grammy make ginger bread
Singing, dancing, jumping
No hot dogs please, can we have cheese burgers instead?
No fair! She took my lip gloss
I'm tired of my big sister thinking she the boss
That's enough fighting
Try to get along now
We are all tired out
Time to quiet down
Grammy one more snack please?
Oh no not tonight
Did I hear y'all cough and sneeze?
Cough syrup, bath time and polka dot pajamas
Time to floss and brush y'all teeth
Don't want to hear no more noise of running little feet
We will rise in the morning
Eat breakfast, get dressed and get going
But for now, sweet dreams of unicorns.
And sweet treats that you love the best
Lights off little Butter cup and ladybug say your prayers it's time
to get y'all beauty rest.

To my wonderful grand children.

Addiction and Motherhood
Praying for all of My Strung Out Sisters Deliverance

Strung Out and Sold Out

Sold my soul out for a good high
It cost me everything I loved
I'm hooked and can't stop
Don't know why?
Can't find the strength to tell my heroin addiction good-bye
Woke up so stoned didn't know where I was today
Found out I lost my place and my five babies
Don't what to do now
Ain't got no place to stay

Addiction is real
It's a one side love affair
You love it but it don't love back
A substance with no feelings to care
It's a compelling strong spirit
Every indulge a deadly hit
Every waking moment and breath I take
I wanna to get more lit
Maybe one day I'll get clean and get myself right
But for now, I'm gonna enjoy this high.
Maybe tomorrow I'll fight

BLACK CHILD

Black child, Black child
I can see the innocence through your eyes
I feel your pain and abandonment and the tears you cry
Black child, Black child,
I see you looking for food to eat
Bread, cereal or a piece of meat
Black child, Black child,
I see you looking for your momma, 'cause she ain't in her bed
Last time you saw her, she was out of her head
Black child, Black child,
I see you looking for your Daddy
Cause you ain't seen him lately,
And the last time you did, he said you ain't even his baby
Black child, Black child
I see you cold and all alone, calling for your momma
But ain't no body home
Black child, Black child
Once again, I see my reflection in your eyes
Cause your Momma ain't right and Daddy been gone a while
But grandma ain't forgot you 'cause she loves you black child.

THE SUBSTANCE OF A WOMAN

What manner of creation is woman?
The origin of her being was developed in the lonely heart of man
Her completion was established through Adam's rib and God's
miraculous hand
Entwined with God's spirit and man's inquisitive heart
She is always searching for her reason, her purpose
And always trying to do her part

She is very misunderstood; her motives are often questioned with
suspicion and little trust
And yet those who continue to question her integrity use the
beauty of her femininity as their lame excuse to lust

Her dress is called too short or her eyes are too alluring
She tries to find her inner sensuality, without feeling
Like she is undesirable or too boring

She has so much affection to offer to those who will receive her love

She is spiritual, gifted and morally strong, with all of the
versatility and values that God has instilled in her to help to keep
her family from straying away and doing wrong

She loves her God, supports her man, and raises her family too
And if that's not enough she helps to raise her children's children
and even sometimes... her grand children's children and the list go
on and y'all know it's true

Time for herself seldom comes around
Because her house is always filled with children and always noisy
in sound

She will work a full time job, come home, cook and clean
Chastise her children to get her home back in order
And yes, sometimes mother has to get a little... mean
What manner of creation is... woman?
You ask me? And I will tell you...
She is one... awesome creation!

Church Lady

Tilted brimmed hat over shadowed her left eye
Humble and sweet but definitely not shy
Gracefully entered the service
Dimpled side couldn't help but be cute
Expensive diamond ring on her finger you couldn't dispute
Usher seated her on the fourth pew in her Donna Vinci suit

Crossed legs in her Tamara Mellon pumps in gray
The fragrance of her Gucci perfume and beauty
Made every woman look her way
They watched her with envy, hatred and gloom
As songs of praise and worship filled the church sanctuary room

The Minister began to preach
And when he presented the altar call
She raised her hand as she praised God and stood up tall
Slipped out of her seat and quietly made her way up front
To surrender it all

When the preacher started talking about repentance and seeing
God's glory
The lady yelled out with tears running down her face
And said, y'all don't know my story
More than superficial things I possess and I have enjoyed
My greatest desire is for the Lord to heal and deliver me and to
fill this empty void

Y'all see a year ago today, I loss my loving spouse and if that wasn't enough

I have a foreclosure on our house and it don't stop there

Yesterday I found out I'm in stage four breast cancer

My doctor's are trying to help but they truly don't have the answer

Pray for me and don't ever judge a book by its cover cause' life can be bitter and sometimes tart,

I'm so glad that God don't look at my outer appearance he looks at my broken heart.

THEN WHY SHOULD I?

Why should I subject myself to your constant disrespect?
Why should I listen to your foolish rhetoric or care what you
think or expect?
If you continue to treat me this way
Then why should I?
Give me one good reason I should comply
When all you do is exaggerate a lie
A painted smile and sugar coated words you speak
You talk real bad about a Sista and call her weak
Be careful what damage comes from your deceitful gossiping lips
Don't think for a minute your little secret is discreet
They tell me the ears you gossiped to the other day mouth leaked
My Sista you need to get your life together and give God a try
Cause' if you don't want be disrespected and break down and cry
Then treat other folks like you want to be treated
If you don't care to do that ...then why should I?

> *The golden rule- (Matthew 7:12- KJV)*
> *"Do unto others as you would have them do unto you"*

Part Five

Children of God

In God's Image

MAN WAS MADE IN GOD'S IMAGE & ALTERED, IN
THIS SPIRITUAL WAR AND STRUGGLE OF SCRIMMAGE

SO, GOD BECAME MAN TO RECREATE THE IMAGE
OF MAN BACK TO HIS VERY OWN...
HE WASN'T TRIPPIN' ABOUT MAN'S NATIONALITY,
HERITAGE OR HIS SKIN TONE

GOD LOVED MAN SO MUCH HE DIED TO SAVE AND TO
REDEEM HIM FROM HIS LIFE OF SIN...TAKE A LOOK IN
THE MIRROR AND SEE WHO'S IMAGE YOU REFLECT
MAKE CHANGES IF YOU'RE NOT SATISFIED
THEN START ALL OVER AGAIN

> *(Genesis 1:27) "God created man in his own
> image, in the image of God created he him, male
> and female created he them."*

GOOD INTENTIONS

No matter how good your intentions
There's no prevention
Of others misconception of your actions
Remember others don't define you
So just keep on loving, keep on giving and keep on living and
being the very best version of YOU

> *(Matthew 7: 1-2) – "Judge not, that ye be not judged. For
> with what judgment ye judge, ye shall be judged and with
> what measure to you mete, it shall be measured to you
> again."*

From Where I Sit...
I Now Stand

From where I sit, I cannot forget
Where my life's journey begin
I can clearly see what you've done for me Jehovah God,
You know my beginning and my end

As I look back over my life at the pain and the foolish decisions
I've made that impacted the direction of my life and deterred my
path from doing it your way.
Lord, it's so hard for me to comprehend why my life didn't end
Undeserving of your merciful grace that covered the darkness of
my sin.
Your agape love I'll never understand, but Lord, I'm so grateful
that you hold this sinner woman's life in the palm of your hand.
You lifted me up from where I sat and it's by your grace that I can
now stand.

When I look at all of the blessings that you have showered down
on me,
All I can say is thank you Jesus most Holy Lord of all
I honor you my Heavenly Father because from where I sit, I
absolutely refuse to forget how you fixed this broken vessel and led
me to the place where repentance and spiritual complacency met.
The best decision I ever made and one that I will never ever regret.

> *(Luke 5:32 KJV) - "I came not to call the righteous, but
> sinners to repentance"*

TROUBLE
DON'T WANT NO PEACE

Trouble don't want no peace
Sounds too nice and sweet
All it knows is hatred and deceit
I'm telling y'all
Trouble don't want no peace
And I tell y'all why... cause' it don't have none
What lies beneath the surface is
Wretched misery undone
Trouble don't want no peace
Cause it don't know no good and ain't even tryin'
Too busy murmuring, complaining
Fault finding, back biting, crying and lying
Accuser of the brethren always starting confusion
Seeking to devour somebody else's peace
By creating disillusion.
I'm tellin' y'all... trouble don't want no peace
Cause peace gets love and love gets harmony
And oh hateful trouble, is mean ugly and ornery
Trouble don't want no peace
It wants destruction of unity, on this it stands alone
Cause love, unity and harmony ain't congruent with its tone
I'm tellin' y'all... that oh trouble don't want no peace
But I sure nuff do! I'm gonna pray that trouble right up outta my
house!
How about you?

God's Gift of Love

In a moment of cogitation
Meditating on the very character of God
Love exceeds
It transcends above all things
For God is love and love begets love
Love does not hurt but instead it heals
Love does not kill, lie or steal
Love does not create wounds
It binds them up
Takes you in and feeds you
And fills your cup
Love is not selfish; it's not resentful
Love does not hate, its color blind;
It does not discriminate
It does not care if you're rich or poor
Love does not take; it continues to give more
It will love you no matter who you are because it's so genuine
No stipulations, it's profoundly gentle & kind
It's purely, authenticated in richness as wine
Love reflects the true beauty of the character of the living God

*"God commended his love toward us, in that, while
we were yet sinners, Christ died for us." (Romans
5:8 KJV)*

OH, MAN OF MINE

Oh, man of mine so gentle and kind
Your lips taste like a rich sweet vintage wine
Our love shall stand throughout the test of time;
I believe God designed you just for me; our positive vibes connect
so perfectly
We put God first and give each other love and respect;
maintaining our strong friendship since the day we met.

We have this special kind of love thing, it's hard to explain
It's sacred and deeper than our wedding rings
If the birds could feel this love they would lift up their voices and
our song they would sing.

Our love is like a floral fragrance in the springtime and it's
sweet as mandarin honey suckle that absorbs the sun's rays and
marinates in a cold drink of sweet lemonade on a hot summer day,
you quench my thirst in every way,
Oh, how I love you sweet man of mine.

This poem is dedicated to my wonderful sweet husband the love of my life

> *(Proverbs 18:22) "He who finds a wife finds a good thing
> and obtains favor from the Lord" (Proverbs 31:28) "Her
> children arise up and call her blessed; her husband also,
> and he praise her.*

Part Six

Faith Walk

WALK ON WATER

IF I ONLY HAD ENOUGH FAITH...I COULD WALK ON
WATER JUST LIKE PETER...
I COULD DO GREAT THINGS IN JESUS NAME
I WOULD PREACH THE GOSPEL LIKE APOSTLE
PAUL, SING LIKE MAHALIA, GIVE BIBLE STUDIES,
HEAL THE ILL, FEED THE POOR AND NEVER EVER
WANT FOR MYSELF ANY MORE...
IF I COULD ONLY INCREASE THE SIZE OF MY
MUSTARD SEED...
MOUNTAINS WOULD MOVE AT MY COMMAND.....
I WOULD BE HUMBLE LIKE JOB, FAITHFUL LIKE
MARY, DEDICATED LIKE MOSES, WISE AS KING
SOLOMON AND REFLECT A CHARACTER MORE,
AND MORE LIKE GOD'S SON JESUS
I COULD BE A GREAT CHRISTIAN LEADER...
IF ONLY I HAD ENOUGH FAITH TO BELIEVE IN THE
IMPOSSIBLE...
....I COULD WALK ON WATER... JUST LIKE PETER!

*(MATTHEW 14:28) –AND PETER ANSWERED
HIM AND SAID, LORD, IF IT BE THOU, BID
ME COME UNTO THEE ON THE WATER...*

*(MATTHEW 14:29) - AND HE SAID, COME
DOWN OUT OF THE SHIP, HE WALKED ON
THE WATER, TO GO TO JESUS.*

TESTIFY

Can I take a moment to testify of God goodness to me? Every waking moment I testify of breath of life I receive, I woke up in my right mind with a voice to speak, movement of my limbs, and he gave me two bright eyes to see.

Food on my table, leftovers in the fridge; Lights on in my house, clothes on my back, shoes on my feet and a warm place to sleep. A husband, children, grandchildren, siblings and a host of relatives too, friends and church family, co-workers and a lot of folks that say …I love you.

I won't complain, I just want to testify of God's goodness in my life continually; He spared my life with his divine protection and I know I am truly blessed; if you want to see a miracle just look at me.

𝓘 𝓐𝓜- IS MY 𝓖𝓞𝓓
AND (𝓘 AM) HIS CHILD

I AM- is my Heavenly Father
Creator of the universe in all of his mighty power
Called by many names, Holy Father, Jehovah God
Told Moses his purpose and mission and placed in his hand a holy rod
His voice was heard like many great waters in sound
Told Moses take the shoes off your feet cause' you're standing on holy ground
Moses asked, "What do I tell your people is thy name?"
Tell them when they pray for deliverance and offer sacrifices of bullock and ram
They are offering up sacrifices, praying and worshipping me... their creator
My name is the great I AM!
God is the same yesterday, today and forever more
He came into my heart one day
I'm so happy I opened up my door
I worship you the God of Moses today
My faith in you no one can take away
I say it boldly and not ashamed to say it proud
I acknowledge every day I live that -I AM -is my Heavenly Father and I am his child

WHEN I TAKE MY REST

On that appointed day that the Lord puts my spirit to rest, I'm going to take my rest; oh, how I look forward to peace that passes all understanding. The kind I have never known in this world of turmoil and confusion that seems to never take a rest from its madness. Asleep I will be and waiting for that great divine morning for it will be a dawn of a new day when I awake from my sleep and begin my eternal rest rejoicing in heaven.

When I take my rest; let the peaceful waters flow and sweet holy quietness cover me with the wings of God's serene loveliness. My mind will no longer be filled with passages from this life or the struggle of living from day to day for all of my troubles will be ended and put away. There will be no remembrance of what was but only a sweet peaceful rest. How I look forward to that day when the Lord decides to give me my rest; I'm going to take my rest and enjoy it. So don't weep for me, instead rejoice for a life lived in the will of God. *(Philippians 1:21)- "For to live is Christ, and to die is gain"*

THE COLOR OF RAIN

The color of rain is reflective catching glimpses of our world in every clear droplet like the flight of beautiful formations of Starlings before settling down at sunset, and white tails in the winter grazing the field for their meal of scraps that nature has left.

Like the toad that loves to absorb the moisture in the mist of the falling rain and heavy down pours that washes away the residue of the day down into the sewer drain

A beautiful couple and guests drenched at their romantic beach wedding ceremony and that poor homeless woman living on the streets cold, dirty depressed, wet and lonely

Children joyfully playing outside in the rain and that wheelchair bound man wet trying to find shelter and catch his breath to get his strength regained, in that same moment a sudden unfortunate fatality is happening in our world somewhere that cannot be explained. Every glimpse of nature and many of our life events are captured in small fragments of color of vigorous animation; sprinkled down on us melded into nature's gaper of showery precipitation. In essence, the color of rain is the beauty and pernicious moments of people, places and things positive and negative captured in the atmosphere of God's falling tears.

RAINBOW

Lifted, gifted, noble, humble child of God; encouraged not discouraged some may even call you odd.

For out of your rain came the caterpillar transformed into the beauty of a butterfly awakened from her sleep; from trials and hopelessness to ardent fierce victory leap.

Colors of spring came from out of your fall; lessons from life strengthened you and defined you right before your enemies crumbling wall. Bright child of God keep on shining living out your purpose; for there is a crown of gold waiting for you in that glory land of purchase.

(James 1:12) "Blessed is he who perseveres under trial; for once he has been approved, he will receive the crown of life which the Lord has promised to those who love him."

About the Author

D Holland

A Marylander, a Christian, a wife, a mother and a grandmother, An Innovator, a Narrative Poet, Writer, Playwright, Singer, Actor, and Women's Ministry Leader, She enjoys people, she loves performing the spoken word, encouraging others, reading, she enjoys TCM Classic movies, crocheting, arts & crafts, performing arts, visual arts, sketching, coordinating programs, evangelism and outreach, she also enjoys music genre such as, instrumental folk, gospel, classical, acoustic and jazz. She enjoys nature and loves spending quiet time with God, relaxing with her husband and enjoys spending time with her family, especially quality time with her grand children.

Devora believes her sole purpose in this life is to be a encourager and to shine new light to others just as the meaning of her Hebrew name is **"Bee"** just like a bee she is armed with the word of God, housed by his divine covering, reproduced through innovation as a bee with the gifts and abilities given to her by God, as the bee speaks their language to communicate with each other to build and protect and connect in their communities, she speaks a language of her personal faith, experience, love and unity and healing to others through her kindness and perseverance and as the bee cares for their own, she cares and nurtures her family. As the bee produce and feed on honey, God is the sweetness of the honey in her honey comb (Psalm 119:103). She says, "Oh Taste and see that the Lord is good, blessed is the one that trust in him. (Psalm 34:8-10)

Author's Work

Devora has written and directed local Church plays,

"Adam Where Art Thou?" "Through the Eyes of Eve",

"Hush…Somebody's calling your name"
"What Color Is Your Love".

(Local church commentaries in Monthly news letter)

I would like to take the time now to thank everyone that purchased and supported this book project. God bless you,

The Author

CPSIA information can be obtained
at www.ICGtesting.com
Printed in the USA
BVHW071418110319
542310BV00010B/1063/P

9 781490 793764